CIM REVISION CARDS

Strategic Marketing in Practice

Maggie Jones of Marketing Knowledge

AMSTERDAM • BOSTON • HEIDELBERG • LONDON • NEW YORK • OXFORD
PARIS • SAN DIEGO • SAN FRANCISCO • SINGAPORE • SYDNEY • TOKYO

Butterworth-Heinemann is an imprint of Elsevier

ELSEVIER

B
H

Butterworth-Heinemann is an imprint of Elsevier
Linacre House, Jordan Hill, Oxford OX2 8DP
30 Corporate Drive, Suite 400, Burlington, MA 01803

First published 2008

Permissions may be sought directly from Elsevier's Science & Technology Rights Department in Oxford, UK: phone: (+44) (0) 1865 843830; fax: (+44) (0) 1865 853333; e-mail: permissions @ elsevier.co.uk. You may also complete your request on-line via the Elsevier homepage (http://www.elsevier.com), by selecting 'Customer Support' and then 'Obtaining Permissions'.

British Library Cataloguing in Publication Data
A catalogue record for this book is available from the British Library

ISBN-13: 978-0-7506-8646-4

For information on all Butterworth-Heinemann publications visit our web site at http://books.elsevier.com

Printed and bound in Spain

08 09 10 10 9 8 7 6 5 4 3 2 1

TABLE OF CONTENTS

PREFACE

Welcome to the CIM Revision Cards from Elsevier/Butterworth–Heinemann. We hope you will find these useful to revise for your CIM exam. The cards are designed to be used in conjunction with the CIM Coursebooks from Elsevier/Butterworth–Heinemann, and have been written specifically with revision in mind. They also serve as invaluable reviews of the complete modules, perfect for those studying via the assignment route.

■ Learning outcomes at the start of each chapter identify the main points

■ Key topics are summarized, helping you commit the information to memory quickly and easily

■ Examination and revision tips are provided to give extra guidance when preparing for the exam

■ Key diagrams are featured to aid the learning process

■ The compact size ensures the cards are easily transportable, so you can revise any time, anywhere.

To get the most of your revision cards, try to look over them as frequently as you can when taking your CIM course. When read alongside the Coursebook they serve as the ideal companion to the main text. Good luck – we wish you every success with your CIM qualification!

INTRODUCTION TO STRATEGIC MARKETING IN PRACTICE

LEARNING OUTCOMES

➡ Identify and critically evaluate marketing issues within various environments, utilising a wide variety of marketing techniques, concepts and models.

➡ Assess the relevance of, and opportunities presented by, contemporary marketing issues within any given scenario including innovations in marketing.

➡ Identify and critically evaluate various options available within given constraints and apply competitive positioning strategies, justifying any decisions taken.

➡ Formulate and present a creative, customer-focused and innovative competitive strategy for any given context, incorporating relevant investment decisions, appropriate control aspects and contingency plans.

➡ Demonstrate an understanding of the direction and management of marketing activities as part of the implementation of strategic direction, taking into account business intelligence requirements, marketing processes, resources, markets and the company vision.

LEARNING OUTCOMES – CONTINUED

➡ Promote and facilitate the adoption and maintenance of a strong market and customer orientation with measurable metrics.
➡ Synthesise various strands of knowledge and skills from the different syllabus modules effectively in developing an effective solution for any given context.

Aim

Marketing has to be firmly rooted in theory and practice. Practice informs theory and vice versa. Strategic Marketing in Practice not only builds on the knowledge and skills developed in the preceding modules, but also looks for an overall competence in marketing that encompasses all the various subject areas covered in the lower qualification levels. As marketing is constantly evolving, one of the aims of this module is to explore the latest trends and innovations relevant to marketers operating at a strategic level within organizations. There is no specific syllabus for this subjects as it is based upon the syllabi for the other post-graduate modules and as such draws on all knowledge gained within those modules.

Analysis and Evaluation – Covers the concepts, techniques and models involved in developing a detailed understanding of the market, customers and competitive environment externally and internally the organization, its capabilities, assets and opportunities available.

Strategic Marketing Decisions – Covers the concepts, techniques and models involved in formulating a customer-focused competitive business or corporate strategy and developing a specific and differentiated competitive position. It includes investment decisions affecting marketing assets.

Managing Marketing Performance – Covers the implementation stage of the strategy. This encompasses managing marketing teams, managing change, implementing strategy through marketing activites and working with other departments and using measurement as the basis for improvement.

Fig. 1.1. Strategic Marketing in Practice and links with other modules.

Marketing drives the business agenda

Marketing is a set of activities concerned with creating value for shareholders and other stakeholders by creating and capturing exceptional value for customers. Organizations expect professional marketers to take increasing ownership for the whole customer experience; this requires them to be more aware of the operational business agenda.

Professional marketers in publicly quoted or limited companies have to:

- ■ **Focus on the long term** – While other business functions can maximise economic profit through efficiency, marketing is the only way to create value. Marketing typically creates three times more value than other functions.

- ■ **Create and capture value for customers** – Marketers create the value perceived by customers for an organizations products and services. By increasing perceived value, marketers create the opportunity for premium pricing through which economic profit is increased.

- ■ **Take charge of the business agenda** – Marketing uses its activities and assets to create customer value. Shareholders measure the value that the business has created for them as the sum of dividends paid and increase in share price. Marketing has to take charge of investment in marketing assets and the activities that create value.

Marketing activities in organizations can be grouped broadly into four models:

Sales Support

Common in SME's and some B2B contexts the emphasis is essentially reactive with marketing supporting a direct sales force and including activities such as tele-marketing and responding to inquiries.

Marketing Communications

Marketing promotes through push and pull communications promoting the organization. More proactive approach uses communication methods to raise awareness, generate leads and take orders.

Operational Marketing

Marketing supports the organization with a co-ordinated range of activities. Planning is at the operational and functional level typically used in FMCG, B2C and B2B

Strategic Marketing

Emphasis on creating value and developing a competitive strategy. Practiced in larger and customer-focused organizations with strategic marketing decisions being made by professional marketers or business leaders.

Marketing contributes to corporate and business plans and develops its own functional plan at an operational level.

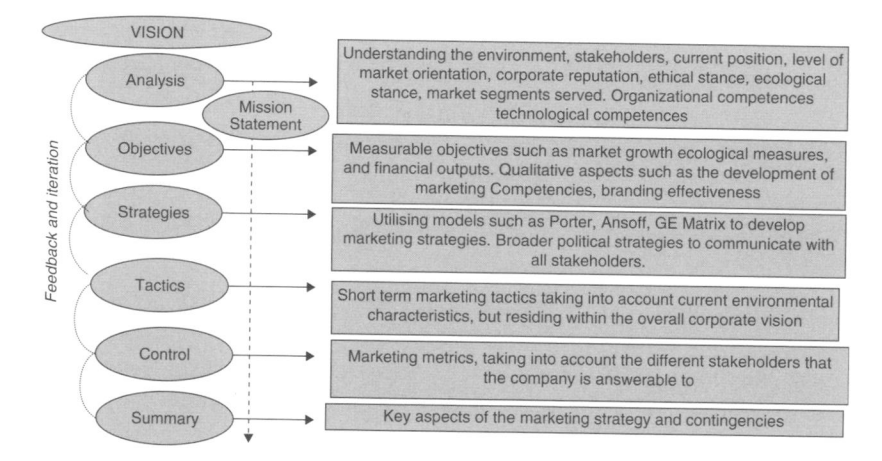

Fig. 1.2. Strategic Marketing model for the 21st century.

Areas of focus for SMIP

The SMIP module is designed to test the application of knowledge gained within the other three Post-graduate modules, alongside the more contemporary marketing issues that effect a range of marketing activities. These include the following:

Globalisation

Many multinationals have operated globally for years but technology is driving change enabling smaller companies the opportunity of operating globally. The introduction of the Euro has lead to the Development of pan-European markets.

Organizational issues

The culture and nature of the organization can lead to the success or failure of the planned marketing strategy due to inappropriate structures or personnel.

Sustainability

Increased concerns over climatic change and environmental deterioration are of critical importance to marketers. It is important that constraints imposed by the environment are considered. Corporate Social Responsibilty (CSR) in relation to the way the organization interacts with the environment and its wider stakeholders also needs to be considered.

Constraints

Resources available, either financial or HR related, can significantly restrict an organization's ability to react within its market sector. A sound knowledge of basic financial statements is essential.

Guidelines for pre-prepared work

SMIP students receive case study 4 weeks prior to the examination date.

Students are required to produce six pages of prepared analysis which will be submitted with the examination script.

25% of marks can be awarded for this analysis as follows:

10% for originality and appropriateness of pre-prepared analysis.

15% for appropriate application of the analysis within the exam script.

Analysis should demonstrate

- The use of models and concepts applied to the case material
- Key issues arising from the analysis of the case material
- An individual approach to the case study supplied
- Clear knowledge of the most appropriate techniques applicable to the case study organization.

Revision tips

- Familiarise yourself with the information gained within the other modules you have studied at Post Graduate level.

- Familiarise yourself with the more operational concepts at Professional Certificate level that you may not have studied formally such as marketing Research and communications planning.

- Consider the range of contemporary marketing issues that are applicable to case study organization and the likely constraints these may impose.

- Ensure that relevant financial and marketing metrics are utilised within the analysis process.

- Remember to cross-refer your work in the examination to the pre-prepared analysis.

WHAT IS MEANT BY CASE STUDY ANALYSIS?

KNOWLEDGE AND SKILL REQUIREMENTS

1.1 Analysis, interpretation, evaluation and synthesis of information, including the ability to draw conclusions
1.2 Identification, exploration and evaluation of strategic options
1.3 Selection and justification of an appropriate option using decision criteria
1.4 Establishing the activities, resources and schedule needed to implement the chosen strategy
1.5 Working with others to implement and control the strategy.

Syllabus References: 1.1–1.5

Analysing the case study

Analysing the situation the organization finds itself in through the use of key concepts sourced from the other Post-graduate modules. Detailed and effective analysis should cover

- The key historical events
- A PESTLE analysis
- A SWOT analysis
- Product Marketing Analysis/Service Provision Analysis
- Issues specific to the Case
- Likely constraints
- Any structural features/control issues
- Key issues arising from analysis

Historical events

It is important to analyse the key critical events which have shaped the company's development. Understanding the evolution of an industry and the decisions made over time can provide a valuable insight into the organization's likely capabilities in the future.

PESTLE analysis

To understand the effect of the MACRO environment upon the industry sector and to highlight key trends, include

- Political factors
- Economic factors
- Social factors
- Technological factors
- Environmental factors
- Legal factors

SWOT analysis

Once the previous two stages have been completed, the information to complete a SWOT analysis can be obtained from Porter's five Forces Model.

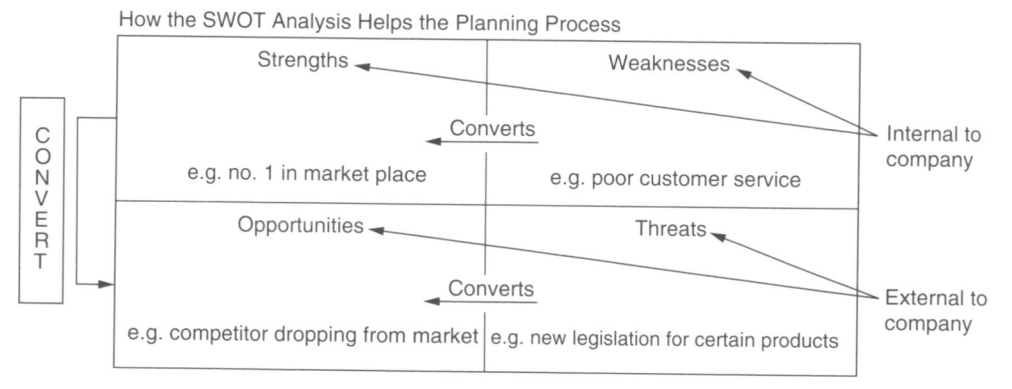

Fig. 2.1.

Porter's five Forces Model

This model incorporates the effect of the MICRO environment alongside MACRO forces.

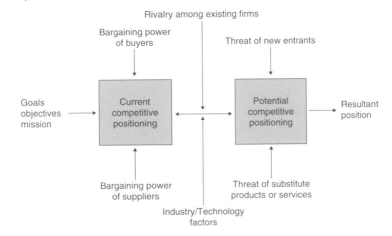

Fig. 2.2.

McKinseys – 7-s model

The internal strengths and weaknesses of the organization can be assessed using the following model.

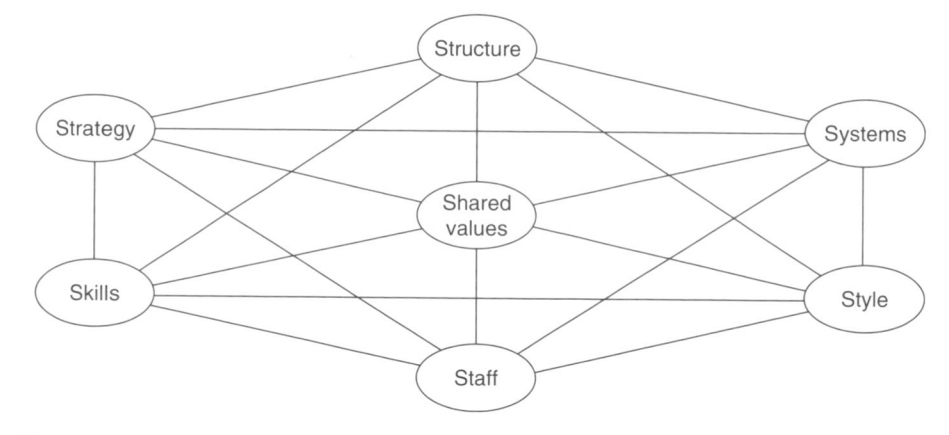

Fig. 2.3.

Product market analysis

Many models exist to audit the range of markets, products and services that an organization is involved in. The first of these are the Product Portfolio models which allow analysis of products or SBUs in terms of the attractiveness of the market and the organization's relative position within that market. There are five models within this category which vary in complexity and applicability.

All can be used as audit tools and for evaluating strategic options later in the planning process.

Boston consulting grid

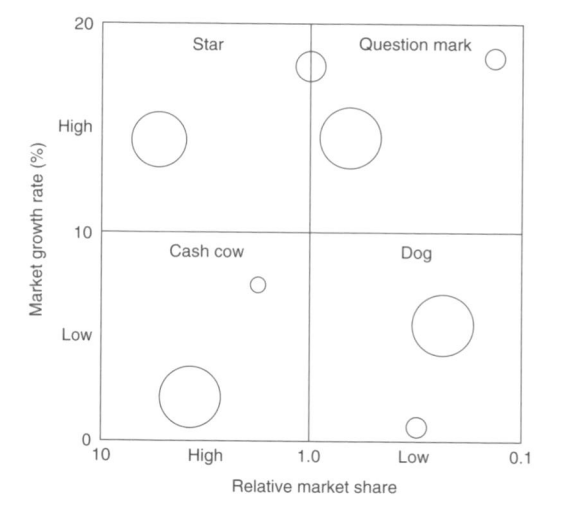

Fig. 2.4.

GE matrix

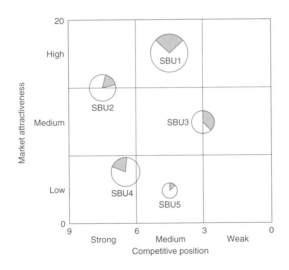

Fig. 2.5.

Shell directional policy matrix

Prospects for sector profitability

		Unattractive	Average	Attractive
Company's competitive capability	**Weak**	Disinvest	Phased withdrawal **Custodial**	Double or quit
	Average	Phased withdrawal	Custodial **Growth**	Try harder
	Strong	Cash generation	Growth **Leader**	Leader

Fig. 2.6.

Abel and Hammond 3 × 3 investment opportunity matrix

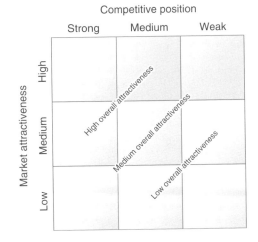

Fig. 2.7.
Source: Wilson and Gilligan (2006). *Strategic Marketing Management* (third edition). Oxford: Elsevier.

The Arthur D Little strategic condition matrix

Competitive position	Embryonic	Growth	Mature	Ageing
Dominant	• Grow fast • Build barriers • Act offensively	• Grow fast • Defend position leadership • Aim for cost • Act offensively	• Defend position • Increase the importance of cost • Act offensively	• Defend position • Focus • Consider withdrawal
Strong	• Grow fast • Differentiate	• Lower cost • Differentiate • Attack small firms	• Lower cost • Differentiate • Focus	• Harvest
Favourable	• Grow fast • Differentiate	• Lower cost • Differentiate • Attack small firms	• Focus • Differentiate • Hit smaller firms	• Harvest
Tenable	• Grow the industry • Focus	• Hold-on or withdraw • Niche • Aim for growth	• Hold-on or withdraw • Niche	• Withdraw
Weak	• Search for a niche • Attempt to catch others	• Niche or withdraw	• Withdraw	• Withdraw

Stage of industry maturity

Fig. 2.8.

Source: Wilson and Gilligan (2006). *Strategic Marketing Management* (third edition). Oxford: Elsevier.

Product lifecycle portfolio mix

This model combines the life stage of the product/service with the portfolio approach, also considering the investment implications.

	High	Low
Low	'Infants' (negative cash flow)	
Medium	'Stars' (modest positive or negative cash flow)	'Problem children' (large negative cash flow)
Low	'Cash cows' (large positive cash flow)	'Dogs' (modest positive or negative cash flow)
Negative	'War horses' (positive cash flow)	'Dodos' (Negative cash flow)

Market growth (vertical axis)

Relative market share (horizontal axis)

Fig. 2.9.

Strategic position and action evaluation – SPACE analysis

Developed by the BCG Group, this model analyses the organisation's position in regard to four key areas

1. Financial strength
2. Industrial strength
3. Competitive strength
4. Environmental stability

By arriving at an average score for each section are then plotted to arrive at a consolidated strategic position.

This analysis works best for private sector organizations and can be limited in its use for NFP and Public sectors.

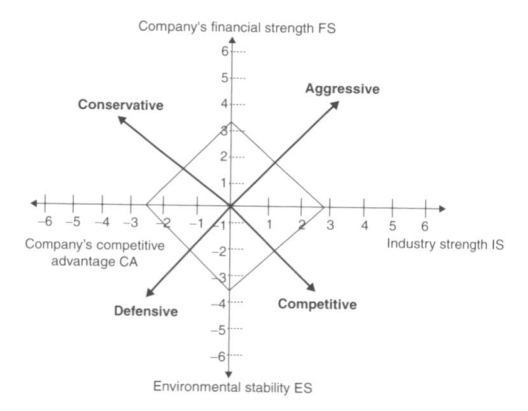

Fig. 2.10.

Factors for SPACE analysis

Table 2.1.

Factors determining financial strength									
Return on investment	Low	0	1	2	3	4	5	6	High
Leverage (Dept to equity ratio)	Low	0	1	2	3	4	5	6	High
Liquidity (cash held)	Low	0	1	2	3	4	5	6	High
Capital required/capital available	High	0	1	2	3	4	5	6	Low
Cash flow	Weak	0	1	2	3	4	5	6	Strong
Ease of exit from the market	Difficult	0	1	2	3	4	5	6	Easy
Risk involved in the business	Low	0	1	2	3	4	5	6	High
Other (your own factor)	Low	0	1	2	3	4	5	6	High

Average:

Critical factors and your assessment of this area of the organization

Table 2.2.

Factors determining competitive advantage									
Market share	Low	0	1	2	3	4	5	6	High
Product/service quality (compared to competitors)	Low	0	1	2	3	4	5	6	High
Product life cycles stages (for range of products/services)	Similar	0	1	2	3	4	5	6	Different
Product/service replacement cycle	Variable	0	1	2	3	4	5	6	Fixed
Customer loyalty	Low	0	1	2	3	4	5	6	High
General utilisation of capacity by the competition	Low	0	1	2	3	4	5	6	High
Technological knowledge and competence	Low	0	1	2	3	4	5	6	High
The degree of vertical integration of the company	Low	0	1	2	3	4	5	6	High
Other (your own factor)	Low	0	1	2	3	4	5	6	High

Average − 6 =

Suppose the total score comes to 36. This divided by 8 factors = 4.5 take away 6 = −1.5 (So you will get a negative score for this factor.)

Critical factors and your assessment of this area of the organization

Table 2.3.

Factors determining industry strength									
Growth potential	Low	0	1	2	3	4	5	6	High
Profit potential	Low	0	1	2	3	4	5	6	High
Financial stability (within the sector)	Low	0	1	2	3	4	5	6	High
Technological know-how (needed to operate within the sector)	Simple	0	1	2	3	4	5	6	Complex
Resource utilisation (generally within the sector)	Poor	0	1	2	3	4	5	6	Good
Capital intensity (requisite capital for operating in the sector)	High	0	1	2	3	4	5	6	Low
Ease of entry into the market	Easy	0	1	2	3	4	5	6	Difficult
Level of productivity and capacity utilisation	Low	0	1	2	3	4	5	6	High
Other (your choice of factor)	Low	0	1	2	3	4	5	6	High
Average:									
Critical factors determining industry strength									

Table 2.4.

Factors determining environmental stability									
Technological changes	Many	0	1	2	3	4	5	6	Few
Rate of inflation	High	0	1	2	3	4	5	6	Low
Variability of demand	High	0	1	2	3	4	5	6	Low
Price range of competing products	Wide	0	1	2	3	4	5	6	Narrow
Barriers to entry into the market	Few	0	1	2	3	4	5	6	Many
Competitive pressure	High	0	1	2	3	4	5	6	Low
Price elasticity of demand	Elastic	0	1	2	3	4	5	6	Inelastic

Other (a factor of your own choice)

Average $- 6 =$

Again for this assessment, suppose the average is 40, this divided by $8 = 5$. Then $5 - 6 = -1$ (a negative figure)

The key critical factors that determine environmental stability

Consolidating the SPACE analysis

The x and y co-ordinates used to position the organization within the matrix are arrived at by adding CA and IS to get the x axis point, then adding the FS and ES to get the y axis point.

The implications for falling in each quadrant being

Aggressive Posture – The company needs to strengthen its position in an attractive market sector which is likely to attract new entrants. This can be achieved by raising Market share or extending product range.

Competitive Posture – Here the company enjoys competitive strength within a turbulent environment. Further strength can be gained by gaining financial strength by reducing costs whilst further differentiating their offering through increased marketing activity.

Conservative Posture – Investment to fund growth is needed either by entering new markets or extending product range. Alternatively, adopting a niche approach can lead to more focus on a sector segment.

Defensive Posture – Retrenchment is necessary where competitive position and financial strength are low. Cutting product lines, costs and slowing down investment are required to reduce the risk of takeover. Turnaround strategies required following a period of harvest.

Gap analysis

A review of gaps that exist to prevent the organization from reaching its goals in the past is also required. This can be achieved

- **Product line gap** – Closing this gap entails completion of a product line, either in width or in depth, by introducing new or improved products.
- **Distribution gap** – This gap can be reduced by expanding the coverage, intensity and exposure of distribution.
- **Usage gap** – To increase usage, a firm needs to induce current non-users to try the product and encourage current users to increase their usage.
- **Competitive gap** – This gap can be closed by making inroads into the market position of direct competitors as well as those who market substitute products.
- **Internationalisation gap** – This gap can be shortened through exporting, joint venture arrangements and strategic alliances.
- **Communications gap** – This gap can be shortened through advertising strategies, PR or proactive use of the web.

The SERVQUAL model

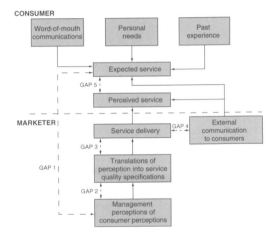

Fig. 2.11.
Source: Berry, Parasuraman and Zeithaml (1994).

The value chain analysis

Through analysis of the process and partners involved within the product/services route to market, opportunities to add value to the customer and improve efficiencies for the organization can be identified.

This can lead to the creation of a Strategic Competitive Advantage (SCA) at the strategy formulation stage. An example of this is Easyjets introduction of a ticketless airline.

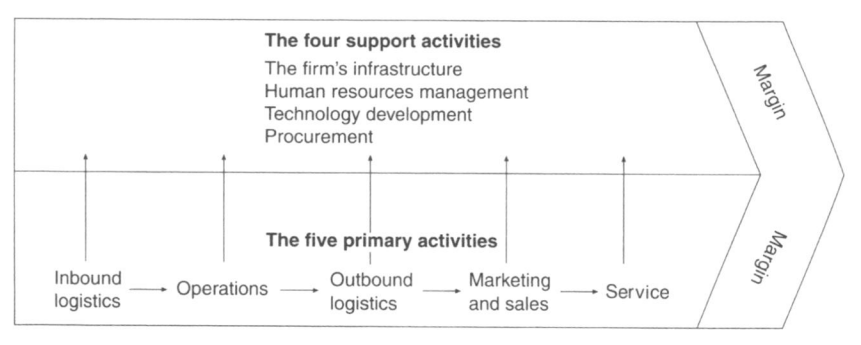

Fig. 2.12. The Value Chain
Source: Porter (1985)

Ansoff growth matrix

One of the first models to be used to assess the viability of strategic options available to the organization, this model demonstrates the opportunities for growth available to the organization.

Product alternatives

	Present products	Improved products	New products
Existing market	Market penetration	Product variants imitations	Product line extension
Expanded market	Aggressive promotion	Market segmentation product	Vertical diversification
New market	Market development	Market extension	Conglomerate diversification

Options

Fig. 2.13. Growth sector analysis.

Constraints

It is important to recognise that future strategic plans must be based upon realistic consideration of the resources available to the organization. These include

■ Market Growth constraints

■ Financial – see Unit 5

■ Technical/systems

■ Environmental

■ Organizational structure/culture

■ HR or skills constraints

■ Other contemporary issues – see Unit 4

Key issues

Through analysis it is possible to evaluate the strategic options available to the organizations.

The Key Strategic Issues (KSI) that have arisen from the audit process will guide this process. At this stage it is possible to begin planning the way forward by summarising the following:

■ Statement of the problem/ KSI

■ Summary Analysis of

◇ Industry data

◇ Product/ service analysis

◇ Financial analysis

◇ Management culture/values

■ Consideration and evaluation of options

■ Recommendations/strategies

■ Resource Implications

■ Implementation, contingency and control

Revision tips

■ When evaluating a case it is important to be systematic in your approach. You cannot move onto assessing strategic options until you are fully conversant with the organization's strengths and weaknesses in all aspects of the business and market sector.

■ Before recommending a strategy it is important to consider if the organization has the resources in place to fully implement that strategy or alternatively build into your plan the means by which those missing resources can be gained.

■ Remember the other Post-graduate modules. To gain a full picture you need to be conversant with all the models and analytical tools used within those modules to fully apply the correct techniques to the chosen case study. Not all models will be applicable to all industry sectors.

UNDERSTANDING THE DIRECTION AND MANAGEMENT OF MARKETING ACTIVITIES

Unit 3

LEARNING OUTCOME

Demonstrate an understanding of the direction and management of marketing activities as part of the implementation of strategic direction, taking into account business intelligence requirements, marketing processes, resources and the company vision

KEY DEFINITION

Knowledge management – systematic management of knowledge gained through rigorous approach to the research and analysis undertaken. It is of paramount importance that the knowledge built is trustworthy, credible and verifiable and that it is accessible to all managers involved in the decision-making process

Knowledge management

In order to make effective decisions, managers must have access to information on which to base those decisions. Knowledge must therefore be both acquired (learning), processed and distributed to those that need it (managing).

The process by which this occurs is reliant upon the following areas:

- The sourcing of information via marketing research
- The availability of information systems to collect store and manipulate information
- The culture of learning to be embedded within an organization to enable managers to reflect, re-evaluate and respond (3R learning) to market challenges
- Monitoring systems and market scanning
- Clear corporate direction and vision

Some of these issues are dealt with in detail under the Marketing Research and Information Module at the Professional Diploma level. As a Post-graduate student it is assumed that knowledge within these areas has been gained through practical experience.

Marketing information systems (MkiS)

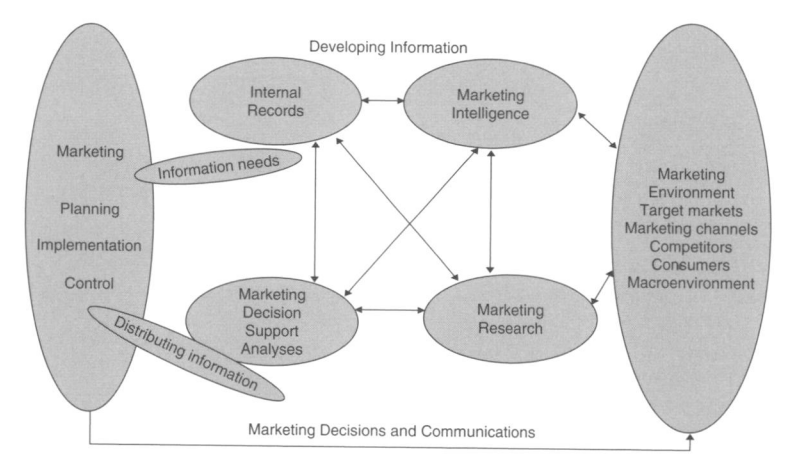

Fig. 3.1.
Source: Adapted from Kotler (1992)

Component parts of the MkiS

Internal records

Sales records, account records and other information that is available within the company. Key issue here is being able to select and manipulate data to inform decisions rather than experience information overload.

Marketing intelligence

Published data is gathered and processed by the MkiS to provide intelligence to aid decision-making. Sources include

- Government agencies
- Business directories
- Trade Associations/journals
- Computerised databases e.g. Reuters
- Published sources e.g. Mintel, Euromonitor
- Competitor intelligence systems e.g. Kompass
- Environmental scanning systems

Decision support systems

Systems and software to process, manipulate and analyse the information from other areas of the MkiS in order to inform decision making e.g. Sensitivity analysis, Statistical modelling and Forecasting techniques.

Marketing research

Secondary research

Information, which exists independently of the organization and was not created specifically for the use of an individual organization.

Sources as detailed under Marketing Intelligence

Secondary data can

- Inform the primary research process
- Chart historical data such as market trends
- Be a cost-effective research method for SMEs and NFP sector

But must also be carefully examined to assess its

- Accuracy
- Reliable
- Valid for the purpose

Primary research

Give insight into behavioural patterns e.g. Product usage, competitive positioning, evolving needs in order to inform the strategy formulation process.

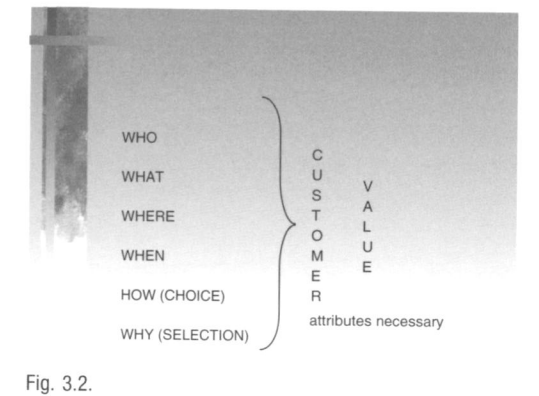

Fig. 3.2.

Competitive strategy as an emergent learning process

Sustainable Competitive Advantage is built upon an organization's ability to adapt to changing conditions by making effective decisions to develop and implement a strategy which delivers superior value to customers.

However, learning is required to acquire and develop the skills, necessary for this process to occur.

> Wilson and Gilligan 2004 suggest the following elements of a **Customer value-based philosophy**
> - A strong market orientation
> - A process of continuous learning
> - A commitment to innovation

> Organizational values for effective learning requirements:
> - A commitment to learning
> - Open mindedness
> - A shared Vision
> - Organizational knowledge sharing

In order to achieve a shared purpose to benefit from learning, the organization often develops a mission statement to express the vision and values of the organization.

Mission statements

Pearce and David (1987) suggested a mission statement should incorporate the following:

- Customers – the target market
- Products/services – offerings and value provided to the customers
- Geographic markets – where the form seeks customers
- Technology – used to produce and market products
- Concern for survival/growth/profits – being financially sound
- Philosophy – values, ethics and beliefs
- Public image – in relation to the contribution made to communities
- Employees – importance of managers and employees
- Distinctive Competence – how is the firm better or different compared to its competitors

The learning organization and market-based learning

The organization can learn in two ways,

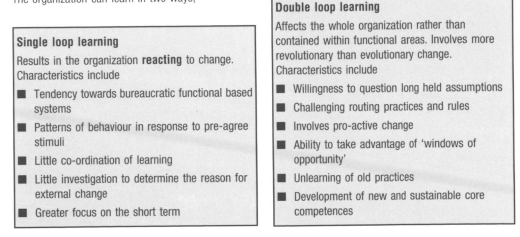

Single loop learning

Results in the organization **reacting** to change. Characteristics include

- Tendency towards bureaucratic functional based systems
- Patterns of behaviour in response to pre-agree stimuli
- Little co-ordination of learning
- Little investigation to determine the reason for external change
- Greater focus on the short term

Double loop learning

Affects the whole organization rather than contained within functional areas. Involves more revolutionary than evolutionary change. Characteristics include

- Willingness to question long held assumptions
- Challenging routing practices and rules
- Involves pro-active change
- Ability to take advantage of 'windows of opportunity'
- Unlearning of old practices
- Development of new and sustainable core competences

The impact of double and single loop learning

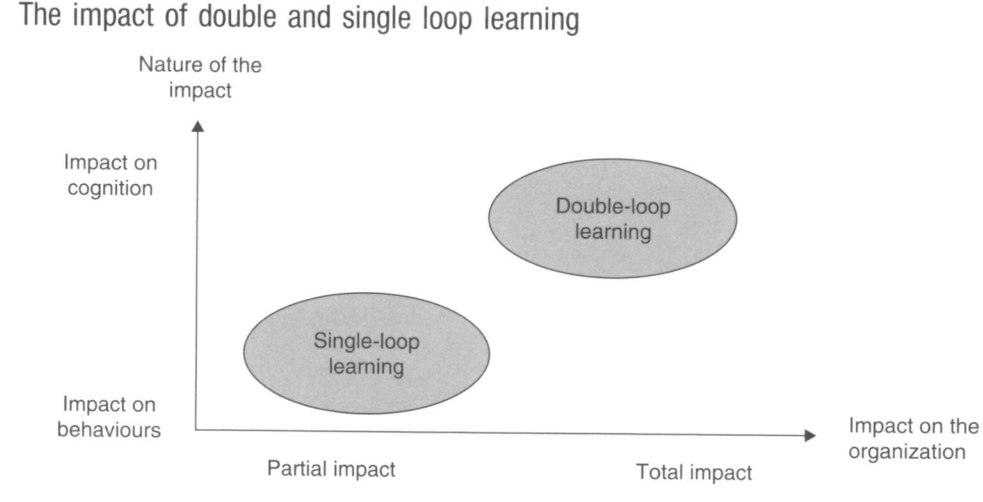

Fig. 3.3.

System and learning

A true learning organization will place great value on Information transmission contributing to general learning. This requires

> **Knowledge Acquisition** – converting data into knowledge that can be understood and assimilated.
>
> **Information distribution** – Distributing information and knowledge throughout the organization.
>
> **Information interpretation** – Understanding the information and interpreting it so that sensible opinions can be formed.
>
> **Organizational memory** – Understanding the new knowledge and embedding it in to the organizations memory.

Market-based learning

Organizations need to learn from the sectors they operate within so that the organizational memory consists of market-based learning.

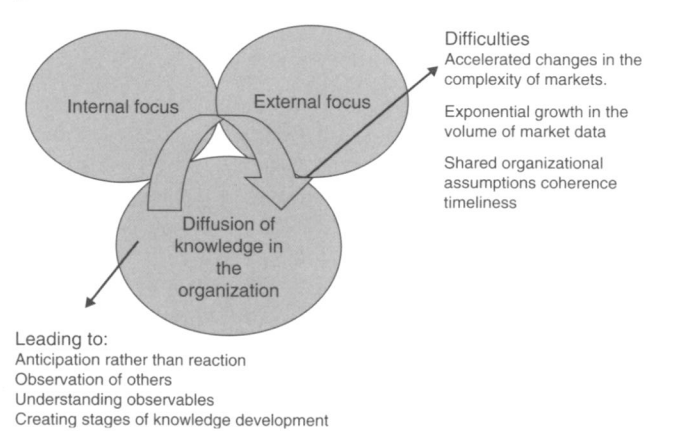

Internal focus

External focus

Diffusion of knowledge in the organization

Difficulties
Accelerated changes in the complexity of markets.

Exponential growth in the volume of market data

Shared organizational assumptions coherence timeliness

Leading to:
Anticipation rather than reaction
Observation of others
Understanding observables
Creating stages of knowledge development

Fig. 3.4.

Revision tips

■ Knowledge and analysis of a number of organizations will enable you to identify how knowledge management and systems can enable organizations to compete on a much higher level.

■ Consider the different management styles and culture that are evident in some of the organizations you know. Compare them with their competitors and analyse the benefits/disadvantages of a range of management styles.

■ Compile a portfolio of articles about organizations spanning all the industry sectors. Analyse their core competences and consider what measures they put in place to deliver those competences.

■ Investigate a range of secondary data to more fully understand the wealth of information that is available.

■ Ensure you are fully conversant with Marketing research techniques to enable you to recommend those required within a given case study.

CONTEMPORARY MARKETING ISSUES

LEARNING OUTCOMES

➡ Assess the relevance of opportunities presented by contemporary marketing issues within any given scenario including innovation in marketing.

BACKGROUND

Students are required to have gained knowledge on a number of environmental factors that are combining to put pressure on the organization. These include

Similarity of Core Products

- Increasing customer awareness
- Increased mergers, alliances and takeovers
- International trade/globalisation

- Increasing customer protection legislation
- Ethical and environmental concerns

Other contemporary marketing issues

- Relationship marketing
- Key Account management
- Sustainability in Marketing
- Corporate identity

Relationship marketing

Marketing is to establish, maintain and enhance relationships with customers and other partners at a profit, so that the objectives of both parties are met. This is achieved by a mutual exchange and fulfilment of promises (Gronroos, 1994).

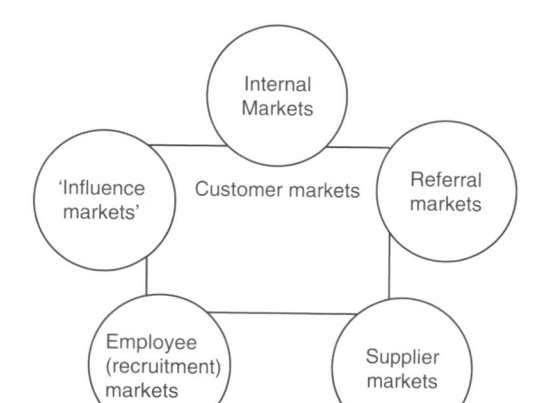

Fig. 4.1.
Source: Christopher et al. (2000) *Relationship Marketing: Bringing Quality, Customer Service and Marketing Together*, Oxford: Butterworth-Heinemann, p. 21.

Essential characteristics

■ **Long-term orientation** – closing the loop between getting customers and keeping them

■ **Ability to communicate and achieve mutually beneficial objectives** – requires a proactive approach with on-going two-way communication

■ **Fulfilment of promises by all concerned** – long term relationships require investment in time, resources, bonding and exclusion of others. Relationship needs to be balanced

Misconceptions about relationship marketing

■ Putting a customer's name on a letter does not constitute a relationship

■ Relationships are not based on convenience but a voluntary patronage where other choices exist

■ It is a philosophy that requires embracing, not just an add on service

■ Everyone should be doing it – relationship marketing is not suitable for all.

■ Restricted to customers – relationships with other stakeholders are just as important

Commitment and trust – Little and Marandi

The extent of relationship marketing

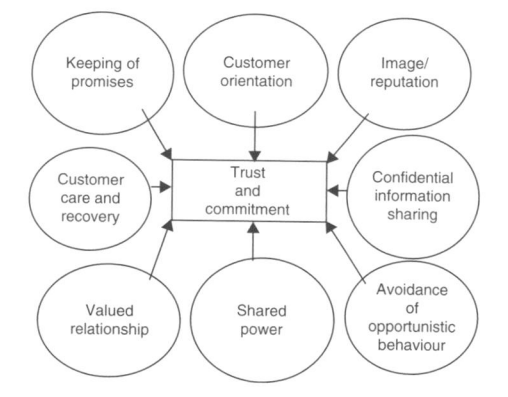

Fig. 4.2.
Source: Little and Marandi (2003).

Key account management (KAM)

A manifestation of relationship marketing in business-to-business markets. The theory and practice of KAM is narrower in scope relating closely to the sales function. Also known as National Account Management (NAM), Strategic account management (SAM) or account management (AM) dependent on industry.

Requires

■ The conscious selection of accounts that are key to future growth/profitability

■ Development and maintenance of long term relationships

■ Establishment of cross functional processes for servicing accounts

Activities undertaken (Homburg et al., 2002)

■ Special pricing

■ Development of special products/services

■ Information sharing

■ Customisation of products and services

■ Joint co-ordination of work flow

■ Taking over customer business processes

The Bow tie structure

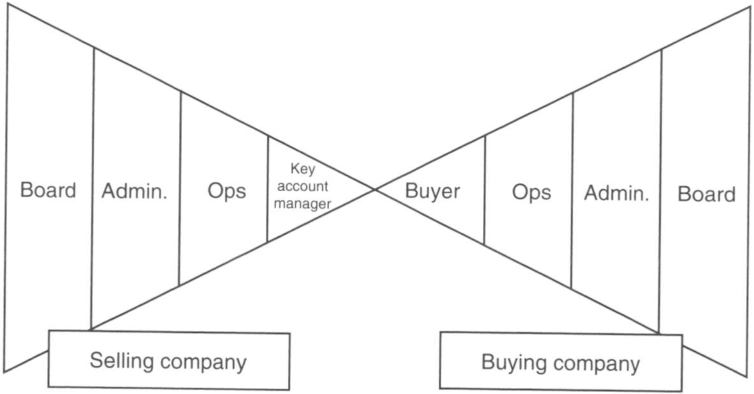

Fig. 4.3.
Source: McDonald, M. (2000) 'key account management – a domain review', *The Marketing Review*, 1, 15–34, Reprinted with permission of Westburn Publishers Ltd

Benefits of KAM

Supplier benefits	Mutual benefits	Buyer benefits
Increased turnover Reduced costs Increased profitability	Risk reduction Shared resources Innovation & learning Social relations	Customised products/ services Price reduction

Fig. 4.4.

Criteria for selecting key accounts

There is a need to agree the selection criteria to ensue both parties are entering into the relationship with similar goals. Criteria include

- Relationship history
- Volume of business
- Profitability
- Inferred status
- Ease/difficulty of replacement
- Resource synergies
- Strategic compatibility

When choosing a key supplier

- Product/service quality
- Ease of doing business
- Calibre of staff

Activities involved in servicing key accounts

- Quality Improvement
- Customisation to closely meet needs
- Conflict resolution and problem-solving in relation to maintaining the relationship
- Information sharing
- Resource sharing
- Communication – frequent two-way informal, but always with a purpose

Sustainability

Maximising profits and looking for short-term gains in market share may be in itself harmful to groups of stakeholders such as employees, local communities and most importantly the planet. Increasingly the public feel that businesses should take responsibility for environmental damage inflicted on the earth and its people.

However the term "green marketing" has many different meanings

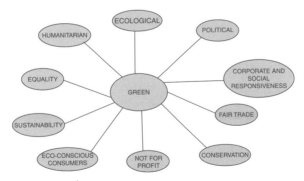

Fig. 4.5.

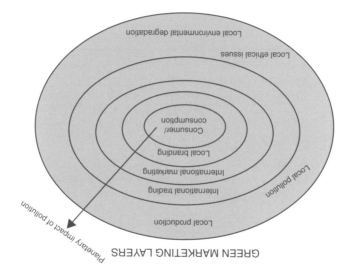

GREEN MARKETING LAYERS

Consumer/consumption

Local branding

International marketing

International trading

Local production

Local pollution

Local environmental degradation

Local ethical issues

Planetary impact of pollution

Fig. 4.6.

Lifecycle analysis (LCA)

An analytical environmental management tool developed by SPOLD (1995) to gain understanding of environmental implications of actions we take. This concept promotes the consideration of Cradle-to grave implications.

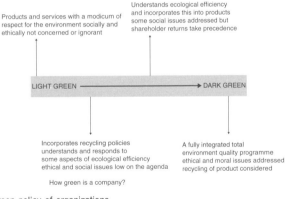

Products and services with a modicum of respect for the environment socially and ethically not concerned or ignorant

Understands ecological efficiency and incorporates this into products some social issues addressed but shareholder returns take precedence

LIGHT GREEN ⟶ DARK GREEN

Incorporates recycling policies understands and responds to some aspects of ecological efficiency ethical and social issues low on the agenda

A fully integrated total environment quality programme ethical and moral issues addressed recycling of product considered

How green is a company?

Fig. 4.7. Measuring the green policy of organizations.
Source: Ranchhod (2001).

Green lifecycle analysis

SPOLD go on to demonstrate that the supply chain or key stakeholders cannot continue to limit their responsibilities to the phases of the life cycle they are involved in The eventual recycling of a component part of a product at the end of its life is the responsibility of the organization making that component.

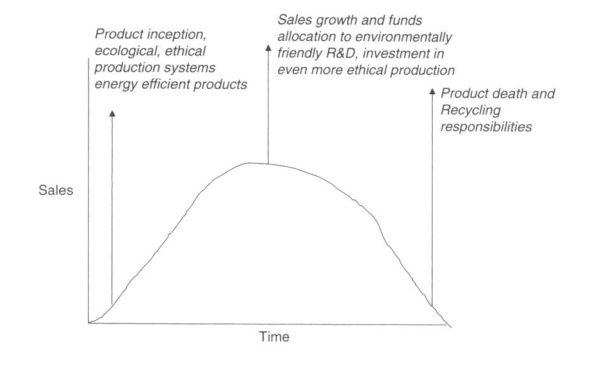

Fig. 4.8.
Source: Ranchhod (2001).

Assessing green credentials

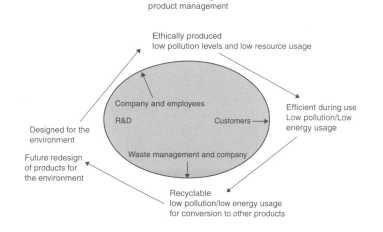

The virtuous, sustainable green circle for product management

Ethically produced
low pollution levels and low resource usage

Company and employees

R&D   Customers →

Efficient during use
Low pollution/Low
energy usage

Designed for the
environment

Future redesign
of products for
the environment

Waste management and company

Recyclable
low pollution/low energy usage
for conversion to other products

Fig. 4.9.

Sustainability and ethical matrix

Developed by understanding of various academic work carried out on green/ethical issues. An average score in response to a series of questions then allows the organization to 'plot' its position on the matrix below. Comparison with competitors and movement over time can also be measured.

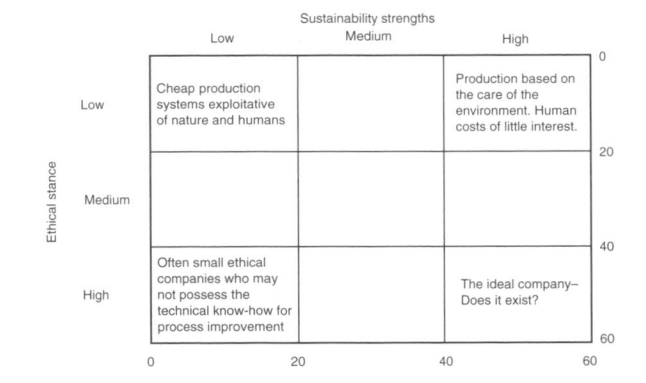

Fig. 4.10.

Green Management questions					
	Very poor	Poor	Adequate	Good	Very good
	1	2	3	4	5
1. Design for the environment					
2. Energy efficiency in manufacturing					
3. Waste in manufacturing					
4. Pollution during manufacturing					
5. Recyclability of packaging					
6. Lifespan of product					
7. Energy efficiency during use					
8. Recyclability of product					
9. Total quality environmental management					
10. Search for new green product opportunities					
11. Use of pollution control equipment					
12. Compliance consulting					

Fig. 4.11.

Ethical considerations	1	2	3	4	5
1. Working conditions					
2. Staff welfare and health care					
3. Limitation of exposure to pollutants					
4. Sustainability of operations within local ecology.					
5. Involvement of stakeholders in environmental issues					
6. Continuous pollution monitoring					
7. Management of the end of the life cycle without affecting others (prevention of dumping in poor area)					
8. Respect for fauna and flora					
9. Adequate compensation to local suppliers					
10. Honesty in advertising					
11. Discussions with NGOs					
12. Environment restoration post production					

Fig. 4.11. Continued

The green shift in organisations

Table 4.1.

Old World View	New World View
Continuous unbridled growth	Sustainable, green economics
Conquer nature, reap resources	Biophilia (affinity for nature)
Environmental compliance	Eco-auditing
Marketing to fill needs	Marketing to sustain life
Materialism	Personalism
Industrial production	Industrial ecology
Design for obsolescence, disposal	Design for environment
Cost accounting (profit/loss statements)	Full cost accounting
Departmentalism, reductionism	Holism

The Green consumer segments

As defined by Roper Starch (Rand Corporation, 2000) in the Green Gauge report

True-Blue Greens – 11% of population. Recyclers, composers, letter writers and volunteers of the world. Go out of their way to buy goods and services with environmentally preferable attributes.

Greenback Greens – 5%. Will contribute to environmental organizations and pay more for green options but will not change lifestyle or housekeeping practices.

Sprouts – 33% – Care about the environment but will only spend slightly more for environmentally sensitive goods.

Grousers – 18% – People who care about the environment but regard it as someone else's problem. Don't seek environmentally sensitive goods or consider lifestyle changes.

Basic browns – 33% – Essentially unconcerned about the environment.

Green consumer behaviour

Factors affecting green consumer behaviour

Knowledge and understanding of environmental issues

Values, motives, desires
Emotions feelings

Ethical, religious, spiritual dimensions

Part of a counter-culture?

GREEN CONSUMER BEHAVIOUR

Cultural climate, influencing it and influenced by

Socio-demographic profile
Age, gender, political affiliation, etc.

Peer group and social network

Lifestyle choice

Impact of media and pressure group campaigns. Impact of crises such as BSE.

Fig. 4.12.
Source: Adapted from Wagner (2001).

Green marketing strategies

In order to gain a competitive advantage organizations have to demonstrate to following characteristics:

- Offering products that address ethical, moral and sustainability issues
- Producing goods which are both commercially viable and meet green customer needs
- Using some profits for environmental and social improvement at the production source.
- Segmenting markets effectively so that consumer needs are understood and targeted accordingly
- Communicating honest and credible messages to all stakeholders
- Ensure the transport and logistics systems employed mirror the organizational green and ethical stance
- Develop a marketing perspective on the cradle-to grave approach
- Offering educational marketing literature where products are complex
- Understanding future needs – monitor trends, carry out research.

Corporate identity

The concept of Corporate Identity is important for the same reason as relationship marketing and branding – the increased competition in the marketplace and the need to differentiate.

The increasing importance of Integrated Marketing communications in associating the organisation with values that can be used to build relationships and develop a corporate personality is also a key.

Three approaches (Olins, 1995)

Graphic design approach – The original notion of corporate identity being linked to visual identity, where visual cues are used to identify and distinguish an organisation from others.

Integrated communications approach – Corporate identity becomes a means of effectively communicating with stakeholders, which often begin with the mission statement and positioning of the organisation.

Synthesis approach – Corporate identity is created through both visual and behavioural strategies and involves an externalisation of an organization's unique traits, capabilities and competencies. A more holistic approach.

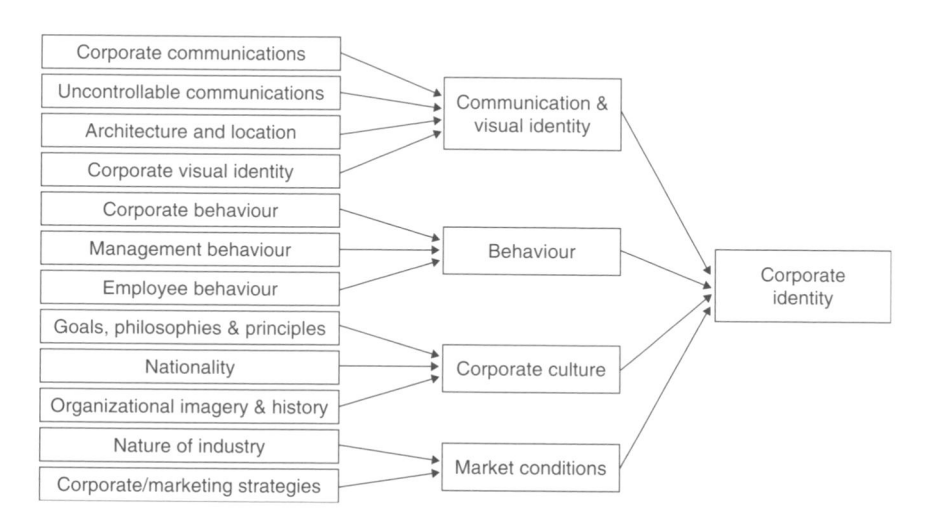

Fig. 4.13.

Branding

Typical definition – The process used by a company to distinguish its products from those of its competitors through assigning a name, term, sign, symbol, packaging and design.

In reality, associations with brands are not just in relation to a name or symbol. They also need to satisfy the emotional and psychological needs of the customer. Brands now enable customers to make lifestyle statements.

Marketing research can enable decision-making concerning:

- What are the physical and emotional benefits to buying a brand?
- In what tangible way is brand A better than brand B?
- Which psychological needs will brand A satisfy better than brand B? How will it do this?
- What are the core values of the brand?
- What are the brand associations linked to the brand, for example, Cadbury/Purple/Heritage/Quality?
- Brand Image – how does the target market perceive the brand e.g. trendy/dowdy?
- Brand Identity – message sent by the owner to the stakeholders, should link with Image perception
- Brand Personality – character of the brand, e.g. Volvo – middle aged
- Brand names – Short, distinctive, easy to pronounce and Global!!!

Branding strategies

Individual branding – different brand names for different products, enabling it to position the brand differently in each market, e.g. Seiko and Pulsar. Expensive to promote but each is separate from those others in the organisation

Corporate branding – Allows a new brand to benefit via corporate association, but failure may damage that long held reputation.

Multi-branding – Individual differentiation of brands to allow for different positioning with one failure having little effect on other brands. Expensive to promote

Range branding – All products in the range carry the same brand name with promotional costs spread across the range. Positioning consistent across the range and a failure of one can effect others e.g. Cadbury ice creams and drinking chocolate

Private branding/own label brands – often known as supermarket brands. Customised product manufactured for the retailer

Generic branding – refers to a product category rather than a company name. Small differentiation possible, compete on price.

Brand licensing – When an organization grants permission to another to use its brand name in return for commission or fee, e.g. CAT clothing.

Brand development strategies

Extension/stretching

Using a successful brand to launch another in a different product category, e.g. Sony – mobile phones

Line extension

New items are added to a product line under the same brand name, e.g. Kit Kat editions

New brand development

Developed for existing or new markets to enable real differentiation e.g. Cillit Bang

Brand revitalisation

Four shapes – Doyle, 1998

Develop New Markets – when existing markets are saturated growth may occur in new geographic markets

Enter New Segments – promote the brand to new segments or industry sectors

Find New Applications – Can revitalise tired old brands, e.g. Lucozade Sport

Increase Brand Usage Rate – making it easier to use or promoting bulk purchase, e.g. BOGOF

Other branding terms

Brand equity – Value of the brand dependent on:

- Level of brand loyalty
- Name
- Awareness
- Perceived quality
- Brand associations
- Patents
- Trademarks
- Channel relationships
- Global presence

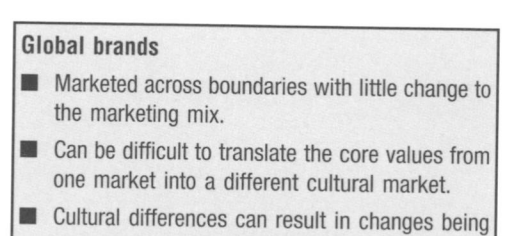

Global brands

- Marketed across boundaries with little change to the marketing mix.
- Can be difficult to translate the core values from one market into a different cultural market.
- Cultural differences can result in changes being necessary to market the brands successfully.

Brand positioning

Relates to the current perception of the brand in the minds of the target customer segment, both as a brand and in relation to the competitor brands in the market.

Positioning is often in relation to the assets and attributes that are associated with the brand.

Re positioning can take two forms

1. Real repositioning – when the product is modified or updated
2. Psychological repositioning – when beliefs about the brand are changed over time through the use of advertising and communications, e.g. Skoda cars

Positioning within a market sector is often demonstrated using perceptual-positioning maps.

Revision tips

■ All of these contemporary marketing issues will need to be considered when you are formulating strategies for your case study organization. Each will have a differing effect upon the selected organisation. Only those, which are important, will need to be part of your submission.

■ It may also be useful to consider the stance of the competitive organizations in relation to contemporary marketing issues and determine if competitive advantages could or have been gained on the basis of these issues.

■ This is not an exhaustive list. Use your own knowledge and experience of a market sector to determine what other issues could be relevant to the chosen industry sector.

■ Look at both the case study and examiners reports for a wider view on contemporary marketing issues – see www.cim.co.uk

EFFECTIVE CUSTOMER ORIENTATION

Unit 5

This chapter will build on the concept of relationship marketing within the customer context as already discussed in the previous chapter covering

➡ Marketing orientation and customer orientation

➡ Details of financial analysis and marketing metrics as control mechanisms

➡ Discussion and formulation of contingency plans.

Marketing orientation is the sum of the specific activities, which translate the philosophy of marketing into reality.

Customer orientation involves understanding customers well enough to create superior value for them continuously.

Inter-functional co-ordination involves the company using all its resources and departments to create value for its target customers.

Marketing orientation constructs

Information generation

Of customer, market and competitor related information as a result of the company's intelligence gathering activities.

The information is either from internal or external sources.

Information dissemination

Dissemination of information obtained to the individuals operating within the organization.

If information dissemination is poor it is difficult for the company to develop the correct strategy for a given market or customer group.

Implementation and response

A company needs to act on the information received, in a clear precise manner. The type of information gathered and the speed of dissemination play an important role on the organizations ability to determine and implement strategies effectively.

Components of marketing orientation

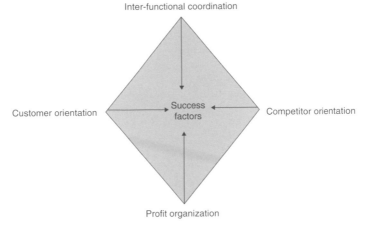

Fig. 5.1.
Source: After Deng and Dart (1994).

Customer-centric marketing

In order to be customer-centric, marketers need to be able to assess each customer individually and satisfy their needs directly or through a third party.

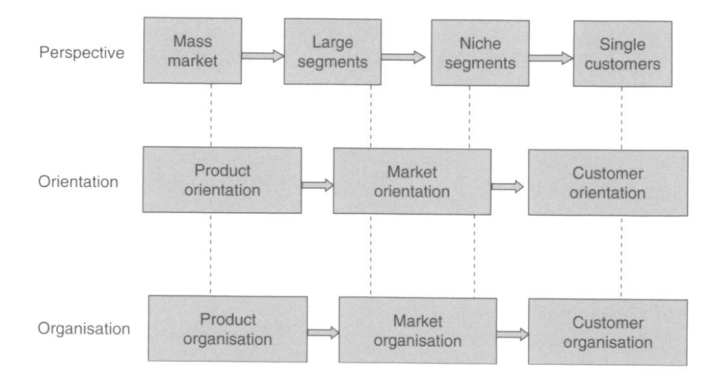

Fig. 5.2. Growth of customer-centric marketing
Source: Sheth et al. (2000).

Customer analysis

Often starts with assessing customer profitability on the basis of Customer Lifetime Value (CLV), which is a controversial concept amongst marketing theorists.

The measurement of CLV needs to take into account the total financial contribution (revenues - costs) of a customer over their entire life of a business relationship with the company.

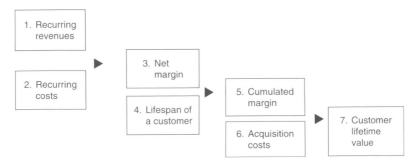

Fig. 5.3. Seven-step process to measure customer value.

Defining a customer unit

Table 5.1.

Number of customers	Number of transactions	Level of involvement
Large	Large	High
Medium	Medium	Medium
Small	Small	Low

Taking the table above, by combining the characteristics it is possible to see;

An organization with a SMALL number of customers, which make a SMALL number of transactions that require a HIGH level of company–customer involvement would define the customer unit as a SINGLE customer or organization.

An organization with a LARGE number of customers making a LARGE amount of transactions would require a LOW level of involvement might find it more appropriate to aggregate the individual customers into segments with homogenous profiles and behaviour. This type of segmentation helps the organization to be more customer-focused into a sensible profit manner.

Segmentation and satisfaction

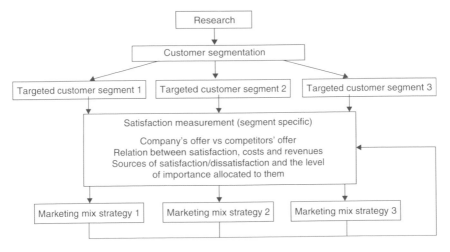

Fig. 5.4.

Basis for segmentation

Any basis used must be:

- Measurable
- Substantial
- Accessible

Consumer bases	Industrial bases
Demographics	Industry type
Socioeconomic	Size of the organization
Geographic	Geographic
Personality and lifestyle	User status
Frequency of use	Usage rate
Benefits sought	Benefits sought

Financial analysis

To disseminate information to shareholders and stakeholders companies produce annual accounts explaining financial flows, profits and losses and balance sheets. In a ratio form these measures are at their most useful to interpret financial statements of the organization and their competitors and can be helpful in identifying trends and highlighting strengths and weaknesses over time.

These fall into five basic categories

1. Profitability ratios
2. Liquidity Ratios
3. Asset utilisation ratios
4. Capital structure ratios
5. Investor ratios

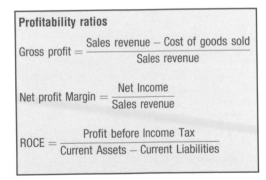

Profitability ratios

$$\text{Gross profit} = \frac{\text{Sales revenue} - \text{Cost of goods sold}}{\text{Sales revenue}}$$

$$\text{Net profit Margin} = \frac{\text{Net Income}}{\text{Sales revenue}}$$

$$\text{ROCE} = \frac{\text{Profit before Income Tax}}{\text{Current Assets} - \text{Current Liabilities}}$$

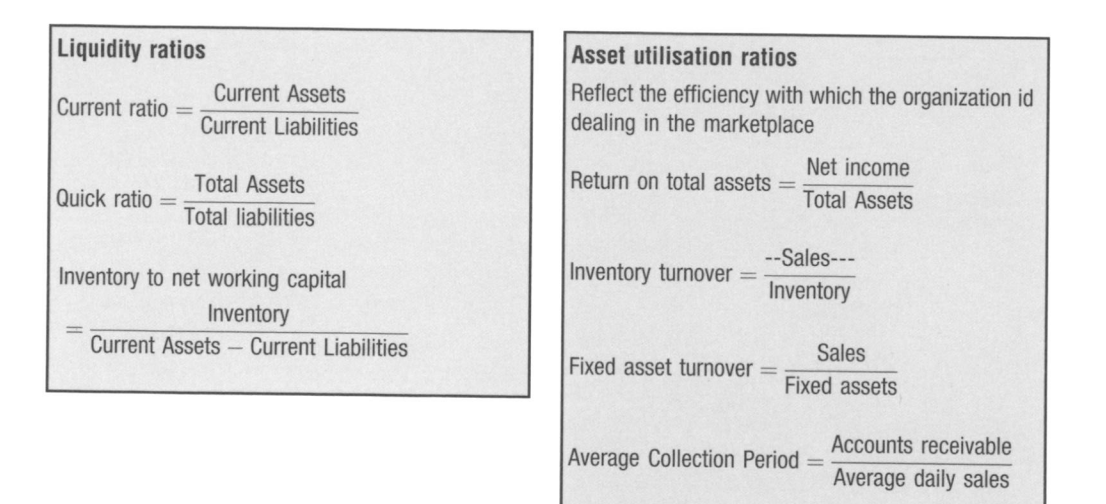

Liquidity ratios

$$\text{Current ratio} = \frac{\text{Current Assets}}{\text{Current Liabilities}}$$

$$\text{Quick ratio} = \frac{\text{Total Assets}}{\text{Total liabilities}}$$

Inventory to net working capital

$$= \frac{\text{Inventory}}{\text{Current Assets} - \text{Current Liabilities}}$$

Asset utilisation ratios

Reflect the efficiency with which the organization id dealing in the marketplace

$$\text{Return on total assets} = \frac{\text{Net income}}{\text{Total Assets}}$$

$$\text{Inventory turnover} = \frac{\text{--Sales---}}{\text{Inventory}}$$

$$\text{Fixed asset turnover} = \frac{\text{Sales}}{\text{Fixed assets}}$$

$$\text{Average Collection Period} = \frac{\text{Accounts receivable}}{\text{Average daily sales}}$$

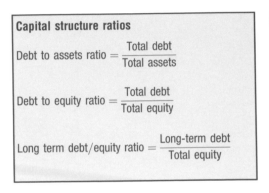

Capital structure ratios

$$\text{Debt to assets ratio} = \frac{\text{Total debt}}{\text{Total assets}}$$

$$\text{Debt to equity ratio} = \frac{\text{Total debt}}{\text{Total equity}}$$

$$\text{Long term debt/equity ratio} = \frac{\text{Long-term debt}}{\text{Total equity}}$$

Profit ratios – Measure the organizations total effectiveness in generating profits from the available resources. It is useful to compare with competitors and overtime to indicate if the organization is improving its performance.

Liquidity ratios – Refer to the ready cash that is available to an organization for its immediate use. The lower the liquidity the greater the danger of not being able to meet cash commitments.

Asset utilisation ratios – Reflect the efficiency with which the organization is dealing in the marketplace in terms cost incurred to facilitate sales.

Capital structure ratios – Are a measure of the amount of debt an organization holds. If investment is required banks will look for a lower figure before loaning capital for growth.

Marketing Metrics

Marketing Metrics have become a point of serious consideration for organizations looking for the best way to measure performance. Having standard metrics for all organizations is difficult so organizations need to assess the most valid model for their specific market sector.

Criteria for choosing suitable metrics

Suitability

- Industry sector/Form
- Orientation of organization
- Level of technological measurement possible
- Visions and values of organization
- Ability to assess trends overtime
- Ability to benchmark versus competition

Feasibility

Does the organization have the resources in terms of systems, information and skills to measure these chosen metrics? What is the cost of measurement, what are the benefits?

Acceptability

Are they acceptable to stakeholder? Are they measuring the correct issues in relation to the organizations stated direction? Are the results tangible and useful?

A framework for marketing metrics

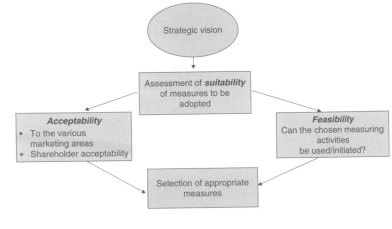

Fig. 5.5.
Source: Ranchhod (2004).

Table 5.2.

Market data	Market size	Market trend
Relative market performance	○ Unit volume trend ○ Market share (volume) ○ Market share by mix by major market segment (value)	○ Relative price levels and trends ○ Sales by major brand (value) ○ Major brand trends (value) ○ Channel (value)
Customer performance	○ Number of customers ○ Customer loyalty ○ Customer complaints ○ Relative quality ○ Relative value	○ Customer service levels ○ Customer satisfaction ○ Consumption per capita (value) ○ Would recommend company or brands to friend
Innovation	○ Activity calendar (past year) ○ New product/service review ○ New products/services launched in past 5 years as % of this year's sales	○ Statement of future opportunities and objectives ○ Partnership, acquisitions, licences
Efficiency	○ Capacity utilisation ○ R&D productivity	○ Awards

People and competency	o % employee turnover o % employees participating in share purchase or profit-sharing	o Training activities, and training spend o Spend as % of sales o Employee satisfaction o Intellectual property
Investment	o R&D priorities and spend as % of sales o Capital expenditure activity and spend as % of sales o Advertising spend as % of sales	o Total marketing spend as % of sales o Technical support to customers
Branding	o Preference o Purchase intent o Brand value o Brand strength	o Awareness o image o Perceived differential o Brand positioning
Distribution	o Level o Trend	o Channel mix o Channel trend

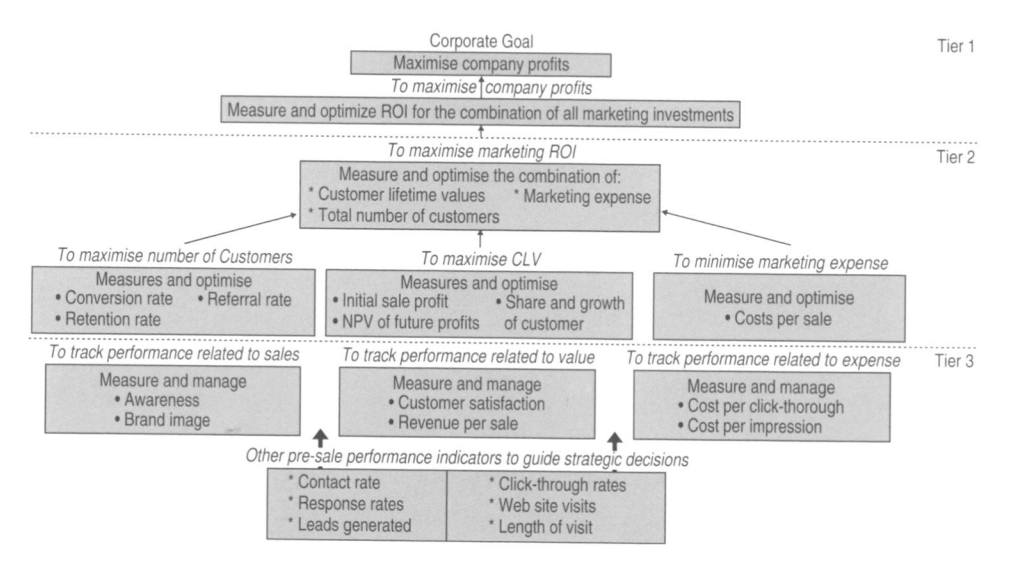

Fig. 5.6.

Contingency planning

In increasingly uncertain and risky environments the need for contingency planning is becoming important. Most organizations do not set budgets aside for these issues and are therefore constrained in acting effectively should a situation arise.

Contingencies are required when
- Supply chain costs rise
- Share of Voice falls
- Price pressure resulting from competitor activity
- Variations in product quality/product recall
- Good or adverse PR occurs
- Changes in technology result in products becoming obsolete
- Internal production problems arise
- Changing external factors. E.g. economic/legal factors

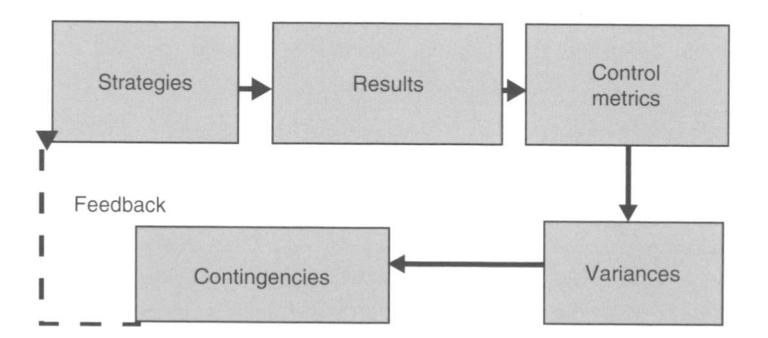

Fig. 5.7.

Revision tips

■ Again it is important to have a detailed knowledge of all industry sectors and sizes in order to be able to develop the correct strategies for the organization. Every organization has its own key issues that it needs to take into account. The case study organization(s) will be no different.

■ It is also necessary to be able to critically evaluate some models and metrics to enable you to justify disregarding them within your analysis. Six pages is not enough to cover all the marketing models available to you. You are marked on the suitability of models and metrics used.

■ The level of contingency planning is also dependent on the sector of the industry the case study organization emanates from. Airline industries are more likely to have a detailed plan in place in comparison to a wool supplier.

■ Knowledge of all financial metrics that are covered in all Post-graduate diploma modules is required. You may find the equations worded slightly differently – revise and remember those that make the most sense to you as an individual. There is also assumed knowledge on terms such as fixed and variable costs, breakeven and contribution – these are often useful in analysis – make sure you are familiar with them.

THE EXAMINATION

Unit 6

LEARNING OUTCOMES

Pulling everything together

➡ How to analyse case studies and formulate good analyses in line with the requirements of SMiP?
➡ How to apply and use analyses in the closed book examination?
➡ What the examiners are looking for?

BACKGROUND

The case study is based on real organizations and candidates are expected to critically analyse it using a range of techniques in preparation for the exam. This is why the case study is sent to students 4 weeks before the exam. Candidates are expected to demonstrate their underpinning knowledge from all Post Graduate modules within the analysis and examination. It is important that creative flair and innovation in approach is demonstrated. An understanding and application of relevant contemporary issues is also required.

■ ■ ■ ■ ■ ■ ■ ■ ■ ■ ■ ■ ■ ■ ■ ■ ■ ■ ■

Skills required for preparing for the SMiP Exam

Analysis and critical thinking

Candidates are required to demonstrate analytical ability, interpretive skills and insight into the organization. The examiner is looking for candidates to take clear and sensible decisions within the context of the case study. A critical awareness of the specific issues involved, relevant theoretical underpinning, attention to detail, coherence and justifications of strategies adopted will also be assessed.

Decision making within context

The candidates need to be competent enough to analyse problems within a marketing context and subsequently take appropriate decisions to implement marketing strategies for an organization. Decisions have to reflect the fact that candidates have thoroughly understood the key marketing issues impinging on the case. They have to make decisions that are realistic, justifiable and actionable within the given constraints of the organization.

Judging between courses of action

There are always several alternatives to a problem. Candidates are expected to pursue courses of action that are possible realistic and sustainable. There is not clear right or wrong answer, examiners look for solutions that will work within the given scenario.

Handling assumptions and inferences

All cases' are based upon real life information that may have gaps within it. No company works in a perfect environment or with perfect information. In most cases students will need to make assumptions. As long as these are not widely off the mark they are acceptable. In some cases students may recommend further research is necessary.

Presenting a point of view

Examiners expect answers to be individual and hence to vary. Group analysis is not accepted and where submitted marks will not be awarded. It is important not to get hung up on what others are thinking, instead concentrate on producing arguments and recommending actions that are justified.

Relating theory to practice

It is essential to demonstrate your knowledge of the underpinning theory through its application in your analysis and answers within the examination. Too often candidates only produce theory or only produce practical recommendations with no links between the two. In order to be successful you need to be knowledgeable about both practical marketing aspects and theoretical issues.

The candidate brief

The brief is an integral part of the case study. It gives an idea of the role you are expected to assume within your analysis and subsequent answers. You will be directed to the key issues you should be considering and some issues, which may be less than important.

The examination

■ Rewards students for work completed between the case study being released and the exam

■ Enables students to concentrate on the case and utilise the prepared analysis effectively

■ 25% of marks are allocated to the pre-prepared analysis in the following proportion
  ◇ 10% for the production of six sides of A4 analysis (Min font 11), submitted with the exam paper
  ◇ 15% for the application of the analysis within the examination. Students should refer to analysis not reproduce

It is important that your six pages only include analysis. Although you are expected to utilise the period before the exam to consider your recommendation on how to move the organization forward these should not be annotated to take into the exam or form part of your analysis submitted.

The best way to prepare for the case

Candidates should undertake the following advice (repeated from Unit 1):

■ Write or print pre-prepared analysis on *six* sides of A4. Examiners will be looking for tables, diagrams and key issues. Tables such as SWOT, though helpful, do not show deep analytical thought.

■ If candidates use the available sheets for writing 'crib' material, such as models or plans they will penalise themselves as there will be less space for good analysis that counts towards the final marks.

■ The diagrams should be clearly visible and the writing should be clearly legible. Typing should be no less than font size 11.

■ Data given within the case should be analysed clearly and effectively.

■ Please not that it will be totally unacceptable for students to present standardised group analysis/appendices and they will therefore be penalised accordingly.

During the examination

You are allowed to take your 6 pages of analysis and your annotated case study booklet into the examination room.

In some cases additional information may be given within the exam paper, which you will need to incorporate into your response to the questions set, and consider the effect of this information on pre-prepared analysis.

In the examination you are expected to draw upon all aspects of the other remaining Post Graduate Diploma modules.

To perform well on the paper, candidates will have to exhibit the following:

■ A need to concentrate on the strategic aspects of marketing underpinned by the necessary detail

■ The ability to identify 'gaps' in the case study and to outline the assumptions made

■ The ability to critically apply relevant models for case analysis

■ The ability to draw and synthesise from any of the diploma subject areas as relevant

■ Concentration on the question set rather than just the pre-prepared analysis

■ The ability to answer in the report format with comprehensive sentences rather than providing simplistic lists

- The judicious use of diagrams for illustrative purposes
- The ability to draw disparate links together and give coherent answers
- The use of interesting and useful articles from journals in their answers
- Developing strategic ideas, centred around contemporary marketing issues
- Innovation and creativity in answering the questions
- Demonstration of practical applications of marketing knowledge
- Sensible use of time and an ability to plan the answers within the set time
- A good understanding of the case study set

The best way to prepare for the case would entail the following considerations:

■ Practice on previous examination papers

■ Reading and digesting the senior examiner's report

■ Reading books, newspapers, relevant marketing and academic journals

■ For each examination case ascertaining the relevant knowledge base that will be required

■ Being flexible and critical when using analytical models instead of being prescriptive

■ Depending on the case study, utilising a range of different analytical models and tools appropriate to the context of the case (see Figure 6.1 for an illustrative schedule for preparing for the examination)

In addition to the above, candidates should also be prepared to undertake the following:

- The use of relevant models for the sector in which the case study is based
- The use of each candidate's practical and business experience using any illustrative examples
- The use of diagrams
- A thorough marketing and financial analysis of each case study within the given context of the case study
- An awareness and application of strategic marketing ideas and solutions
- Revisiting relevant syllabi from the Diploma and Advanced Diploma within the given context of the case study

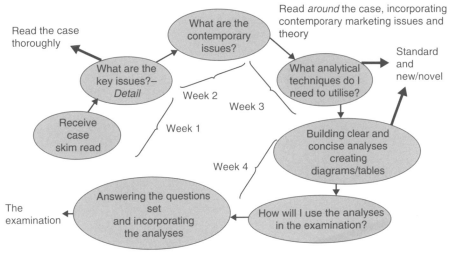

Read the case thoroughly

Read *around* the case, incorporating contemporary marketing issues and theory

What are the contemporary issues?

What are the key issues?– *Detail*

Receive case skim read

Week 1

Week 2

Week 3

What analytical techniques do I need to utilise?

Standard and new/novel

Building clear and concise analyses creating diagrams/tables

Week 4

Answering the questions set and incorporating the analyses

How will I use the analyses in the examination?

The examination

Fig. 6.1.

Conclusion – a few practical tips from the senior examiner

■ Remember to ensure your handwriting is readable and the presentation of your work is in a business like format with headings, sub headings and paragraphs. Use of underlining or highlighters can help make your work more readable.

■ Answer the question set – which requires you to read the question carefully several times and break it into its constituent parts. Consider what is required carefully; make a rough answer plan before committing pen to paper.

■ Do not submit group prepared analysis – marks will not be awarded. Prepare yourself for questions which may be asked, but do not limit yourself by trying to guess too exactly.

■ Include theory where relevant but ensure it is applied in the context of the case.

■ Consider the effect of relevant contemporary issues.

■ Always justify your recommendations. Repetition of case study material does not gain marks.

Further reading

■ Previous case studies and specimen answers available on www.cim.co.uk
■ Senior examiners report detailing the previous candidate's performance available on the CIM website
■ Books, quality newspapers, marketing and academic journals
■ Related websites